*poems of
Italian food
& love*

Saporoso

jennifer barone

drawings by lam khong

for my bello

Also by Jennifer Barone:
Secret City, 2006
Simple Language, 2003

FEATHER PRESS

Published by Feather Press | featherpressbooks.wordpress.com

Third Edition, 2025. First published in 2012, 2017.
Printed in the United States of America

Copyright © 2012, 2017, 2025 by Jennifer Barone
Drawings copyright © 2012 by Lam Khong

All rights reserved. No part of this publication may be reproduced without the express written permission of the author.

For information about permission to reproduce selections from this book, please contact the authors at:
Jennifer Barone: jenniferbarone.wordpress.com / @baronejenn
Lam Khong: followlam@yahoo.com

Library of Congress Cataloging-in-Publication Data

Barone, Jennifer
Saporoso, Poems of Italian Food and Love /
Jennifer Barone, drawings by Lam Khong
1. Barone, Jennifer II. Title

ISBN-13: 978-0-9860231-2-5

*"blessed are the hungry
for they will be fed"*

il menu

antipasti

Love Food	02
Il Plenilunio	03
Il Vino	04
Navigation	06
Il Sale	07
Extra Virgin	08
Il Pane	10
Il Limone	12
L'olio	14
Frutti di Mare	15
I Fichi	17
Il Polpo	18

primi

The Poetry of Pasta	22
Two Spoons	24
L'uovo	25
Le Due Sedie	26
Il Basilico	29
You've Ruined My Pasta	30
Il Sugo	32

La Luna di Miele	34
Even the Tomato is an Immigrant	35
Il Pomodoro	36

secondi

Where Food Comes From	40
Zucchini	43
La Cucina Povera	44
L'aglio	46
Il Peperone	48
I Pinoli	50
La Cipolla	52

dolce

L'affamato	56
La Prugna	58
La Passeggiata	60
La Pesca	62
La Mela	65
Il Nettare	67
Poet Migration	68
Il Cappuccino	71
No Life Without	73
Il Cioccolato	74
La Dolce Vita	75

le ricette	76
le note	78
le biografie	84

antipasti

love food

in the beginning
our first instinct
was a parting of lips
in a joyful "O"

survival and love
existed
with no separation
between them

our small hands
reached for heaven
to know the one
who gave us life
to become
nourished by love

today
not much has changed
we continue to seek
with our senses

when we begin to love
the first meal we share
is tense with this search
for primal intimacy

our favorite dishes
reminscent of the ones
we grew up with

when tasted
sing through every cell
of our body
completely infused with
the memory of love

il plenilunio

tonight I want to serve you a delicious poem
to feed your soul something radical

I contemplate colors, textures, smells
to paint upon your palate
spoonfuls of syllables and fulfilling verse
that will nourish you so much
you must loosen your belt buckle

I bring you my devotion
in the form of a fig
floating my soul on the raft
of its heart shaped halves
to its destiny inside of you

I want to heal your wounds
with strands of words and
strings of honey to sweeten
the sourness of your broken heart
to feed the flame of hidden ecstasy
with crushed red pepper
calm your mind with lavender
coax your inhibitions
with damiana and wine

I wield culinary alchemy
impress your eyes with designs
in geometric patterns of roman broccoli
pair our lives in a juxtaposition
of prosciutto and melon
elevate ourselves in ritual tastings
without leaving our kitchen
from the roots of the earth
to the fruit of the sea

for what else is there
except the pleasure of your company
and two plates between us
licked clean like full moons

il vino

you are the wine and the cup – Rumi

if I am the wine
then let me be
a full bodied Italian red
one that bites and stings
that intoxicates
on the first taste

one that was crafted
at the foot of volcanoes
born of grapes that leapt
from black earth
that sing the song
of sirens
by the Tyrrhenian sea

let me be
the one who carries
twisted olive
and lemon tree roots
to marry
the frutti di mare
on your palate

if I am the wine
then drink me
till the bottle is empty
till your posture softens
and your skin warms
let me work my way
through your body
like a truth serum

and then let me go
having only the impression
of my grape
on your tongue

navigation

we design our life around meals
plotting a course from breakfast to dinner
is a strategic, daily ritual

where to get the best coffee at breakfast
what time to eat lunch and where
mapping our way from plate to plate
requires a special gift for timing
location scouting dictated by taste buds
consideration of who we spend our meals with
what we cook requires creativity and planning
to be unique and complimentary
to what we have already eaten

everything else is just passing time
from one meal to the next
    pleasure
the blessing of nourishment
    satisfaction
not only for the body
but also the soul

religions know
the profound power of this ritual
so much so
that every occasion is marked
by a meal or a special food

even Jesus wanted to be
our bread and our wine

it is no small thing to eat

even if you eat alone
you are never really alone
even those who do not have anything
still need to eat

il sale

I wonder
if you are worth your salt
as they say

I feel for firmness
measure your arms
like a roman soldier
wielding heavy weapons of love
for the salary of my affection

your kisses taste kosher
blessed with pure intention
a flower scraped from
the surface of the sea
when kingdoms went to war
for more flavor

I run my lips
against the bump
of your tattooed bicep
an Egyptian eye
revealed in the sands of time
baked by a feverish sun
you break a sweat

I taste
the salt of the earth
in your body

it makes everything savory
brightens the color of my skin

extra virgin

you threatened
to stand on top of me
and pour olive oil
on my skin

you said it would
heat up
was pure and edible
harmless enough
so your tongue could slide
over my body
gracefully
from one curve
to one slope
down to the valley
where olive trees grow
in no time

among finger leaves
you found
a single olive
awaiting your hand
thick and lost
in brown curls

you threatened to
hang a bottle over my belly
till I overflowed
like an extra virgin fountain

and there would be
nothing I could do
to stop you

sheets imprinted
permanently
with the oily outline
of our bodies

you said the smell
made you think of Italy

but I recall mythology
when the olive was born
in a battle between gods
for the most useful creation

the olive won
hands down

so I suppose
the many uses for olives
could have included
oiling up a lover's breast
or to coax a cock to harden
and ease between greasy thighs
as well as to lie
dotted with balsamic
to dip your daily bread into

but whether from earth or gods
as far as I can see
it seems it has been made
to be poured
liberally
on delicacies
and lovers alike

il pane

to be able to knead
to roll
to pound
your soft and nubile flesh
under naked fingers
to be in and of life
to create

oh bread
let us be grateful

for every living ingredient
in your essence
makes my spirit rise
the heat of existence
expands into the space
of this precious
and precarious moment

your precocious nature
makes you unpredictable
the sight of you
brings us together at the table
where you compliment
everything
dismissing nothing
embracing all

when we hold you in our hands
we hold all that is basic to life
in every tale of great gatherings
you were always there
and always will be

to make you
I become divine
with you I manifest
infinite shapes and forms

I splice the halves of you
like two cells that multiply
knead you with sweet
and savory ingredients
so that every form you embody
is unique from the last
although your base
is basically the same

some flour and water
you are earth and ocean
a movement from my roller
you are air and space
a little push in the oven
at last you are fire
finally transformed

independent of me
you become complete
but at last incomplete
until fresh from the oven
we hover over you
like a newborn babe
running for the first
smell, look, taste of you

oh the glorious sound
of the first crack of bread

il limone

once you grew a pulpy shell
to protect yourself
from heartbreak

a thick coat of flesh
concealed the bright sun
of your innermost self
seeking to be
accepted for your
contradictions

in you I taste
summer in Naples
of times I could suck
lemon ecstasy
from roadside gardens
gratis
savor delicacies
rolled in lemon leaf
drink *limoncello*
under the lingering
southern sun
that romances you
into fruition

only a delicate lover's hand
can bring your fruit to bare
fingers scrape your skin
for strings of zest
disarming
moving forever closer to
this season's hot desire

to finally penetrate
your apprehensive nectar
with tenderness

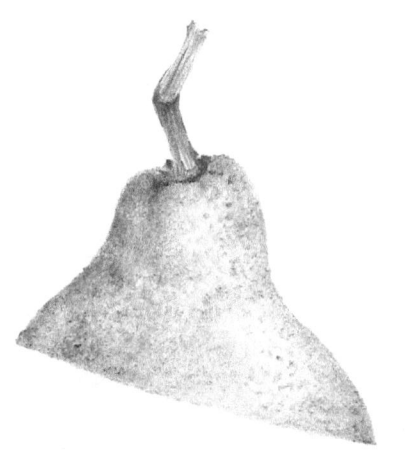

l'olio

I left the apartment
with a stain on my sweater
near my breast

                I can't tell if it was
                from a kiss
                or from oil I spilled
                and rubbed into you

either way
it smells like lavender
so it must have been
the latter
but I won't tell

                I'll let the world
                point it out to me all night
                I'll say I spilled
                something at dinner
                I'll lie

inside
I will know *it was you*
or it could have been me
our sweat
the saliva of a kiss

                either way
                I do not hide
                I wear it
                like a medal

frutti di mare

I bring you
the Mediterranean
seeping salt water into broth
among translucent waves
of tangled onion
and parsley beds

I bring you clam shells
whose lips part
slowly
in a bath
of olive oil and wine
who offer
their tender souls
to you
with a steamy kiss

I bring you sweet
introspective shrimp
who wrap into their
embryonic selves
and curl in vowels of
pink U's and tiny O's

I bring a mermaid's
treasure from the blue
on Neptune's trident fork
for you
my abalone heart

i fichi

I go searching
   under your leaf

     looking for
       the Hanging Gardens
      of Babylon
        between your thighs

         where scrotum swing
          like plump and tender fruit
         that fall in the night

        I have heard
        enlightenment is found
        underneath the Bodhi tree
        where figs dangle
        like monastery bells

      the tree of carnal knowledge
     looms larger than life

   as above
   so below

in my palm
the tender seeds
of your wisdom
wanting to be free

il polpo

when I think of you
I imagine you killing an octopus

like the time you told me
how they were killed
as we whipped around a bend
on the back of your motorcycle

your hand fearlessly left the handle
to point toward twisted rocks off the pier
and fishing boats bumping in the waves
we circled the bay
cars nipped our feet
as we dangled off the cliff

you have to find them deep below the surface, you yelled
    and then a struggle
spiraling arms and suckers fighting off ten fingers
man against beast
my arms gripped your waist

I wondered about your hands touching my skin
would they feel rough like the skin of an octopus
would you tussle with me
fend me off as if I were trying to nab you
from your once peaceful and solitary existence

or would it be easy
like the dinner we were having
full of romantic tension
just you and I
and the fisherman you knew
who served us the catch of the day

you said in order to make an octopus tender
you have to *take it right away from the sea*
    quickly thrust its head against a rock
    WHAM
    slam it down hard
    whip it
    rub it against the rock to soften it
you have to be
    quick and brutal

seeing my apprehension in the rearview mirror
you turned to look at me from the corner of your eye
like a mischievous fish
    no, I'm serious, you said, smiling between words
    sometimes you have to be rough to be tender

as we zoomed past the sea, through a tunnel
your laughter echoing against the walls

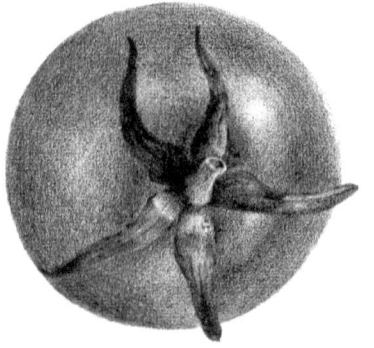

primi

the poetry of pasta

pasta sits upon the shelf
so stable and standard
it may last for centuries
and so it has
and perhaps why I feel
if I don't have pasta in the pantry
that I might starve
as people did
before pasta was invented
    pasta
responsible for the birth of Italy
    pasta
dried on racks in the Napoletane sun
in the town of Torre del Greco
    pasta
hung from volcanic lips
rolled into the sea like molten lava
where ships set sail full of pasta
to feed kings and queens
the dish of the *paesano*
the poor, the hungry
the *mangiamaccheroni*
pasta so strong
it swam all the way
across the Atlantic to America
now everyday we speak
    the poetry of pasta
at the supermarket
    the poetry of pasta
in the kitchen
    the poetry of pasta
written in semolina
from a bubbling cauldron
its story unfurls
if you listen closely —

Cappellini (angel's hair)
wears *Fettuccine* (ribbons)
as *Farfalle* (butterflies)
flutter over *Diavolini* (little devils)
great *Falloni* (phalluses)
heat up the *Lasagne* (kitchen pot)
Alfabeto (alphabet) spells hunger
under *Lune* (moons) *Stelline* (little stars)
Orecchiette (ears) peak
as *Candele* (candles) burn
Occhi di Passero (sparrow's eyes)
watch *Lumache* (snails)
and *Vermicelli* (little worms)
as lovers give *Anelletti* (little rings)
of *Corallo* (coral)
and *Conchiglie* (shells) from the sea
the *Ziti* (bride & groom)
tie the *Gnocchi* (knot)
their love as old as the *Ruote* (wheel)
written with a *Penne* (quill)
next time listen
to what the *Rigatoni* (ridges) are saying
like a record repeating the sound of
    fulfillment
        fulfillment
            fulfillment

two spoons

for Phillip and Elisabeth

two spoons
one inside the other
perfectly rest
in ying yang formation
over two small bowls

one holds
sea salt
the other
course black pepper

spooning

now at rest
one consumes
and the other
is consumed
but neither knows
which is which
or which is better

and so
at night
perhaps they switch
to get to know
each other's pleasure

dishing out
the spice of life
together

endlessly
enhancing
flavors

l'uovo

once violently freed
from fragile shells
with a quick thrust of fingers
against the side of my bowl
two burning suns wobble
in the membrane
of their own universe

    crack
      crack

every new beginning
is thrust upon us

I admire amorphous ovals
how the information
of a young chick
lives inside its jelly
how at some moment
this bright blob
can turn into feathers

the promise of possibility
gets whisked away inside
the womb of my bowl

and inside everyone
amoebas of anticipation
seeds that could spring
another living being
curious cells adrift
in the waters of the body
that might somehow
with the fusion of love
believe they could fly

le due sedie

for Lam Khong

this evening
I was thinking
how much of our
displays of affection
revolve around food
two chairs
and a table between us

for you I will try new things

we argue with our forks
both wanting the other
to gallantly grab the last bite
I say, *no, you first*
I'll feed it to you
or we'll split it in half

once, we ate a bowl of salad
with our bare hands
it tasted much better
fingers full of vinegar

tonight we ordered
chocolate raspberry cake
after Japanese food
I motioned jokingly
to lick the plate clean
its crumbs waiting
we looked both ways
and took our last licks

you order for me in Vietnamese
to surprise me with a dish
pretending not to notice
as I fumble with my chopsticks
I refuse to use a fork
even though it would be easier
I like to entertain you
noodles dribble down my chin

you ask me to read you a poem
I ask to hear one of yours
we struggle to speak and listen
over the clamor of conversations
waiters interrupt us to ask
if we would like anything else

of course not

we take our time
as they begin to close

you steal a flower
from a bouquet in the bathroom
and bring it back to me
I open all its petals
it's in my pocket now
as I return home

this is why I love you

il basilico

sounds like *basilica*
a great place
to pray for a taste

il basilico
opens her lips to the sun
folds in your palm
chopped to blades of grass
that lie baking
in a bed of *Bolognese*

her leaves
were never meant
to hide
but to season
the tender loins
of the first lovers
who wore basil
below and above
their hair like
Caesar

until presto *pesto*
crushed between
a mortar and a pestle

or naked
they lie naturally
like ears over
mozzarella caprese

till I hear you praise
the smell of sweet basil
the leafy earth
on her wings

you've ruined my pasta

all day I have been looking forward
to cooking this pasta with you
our fingers full of greasy olives
a glass of wine
the anticipation of
    your eyes
        and mine
full of culinary satisfaction
    destroyed

you
    want to be
alone
    with your
thoughts

now I am left
eating far less than perfect pasta
with soggy eggplant chunks
and sad tomatoes

worse than adding too much salt
or over-cooking
till it grows limp in your dish
you have made me
    limp
with your willingness to forgo
our rendezvous over a hot stove

what would my ancestors say?
a tradition of pasta
cooked with pride
savored with loved ones
    ignored

I should find you
    break my plate
at your feet and scream
    see what you did to my heritage
    my birthright, my dinner!

but instead
I let you wander in your sorrow
as I stay home mourning
my pitiful pasta
    missing
the most important ingredient
    of your company

il sugo

she learned to make your mother's sauce
because she knew food was the way
to fulfill you and keep you satisfied

in a way she was
taking the place of your mother
when she knew the secret
to making her meatballs
her *braciole*
her stuffed peppers and *arancini*

once when I told you
you needed a real Italian girl
someone who understood you
you told me to go to the store and
return to make you my sauce
as if it were an audition
some test of devotion

standing in the grocery aisles
looking across shelves of canned tomatoes
different brands, different seasonings
I felt petrified

suddenly
I knew I didn't know you so well
because I didn't know your mother
I didn't know how she made *her* sauce
the only sauce that *my* sauce
would most likely be compared to

this was sure to be an epic failure

I remembered my sister who learned
the Sicilian recipes of her mother-in-law
my mother who learned from hers
but now, here I stood without guidance

I wanted to run but instead
I picked up the ingredients and returned

I made the sauce *my* way
I decided if you didn't approve
I didn't care anymore

I was hungry now

and maybe I would never know
the way to your heart
maybe I should never know
because I don't want to be
your mother
whoever she is

I want to be a woman
with a sauce
of my own

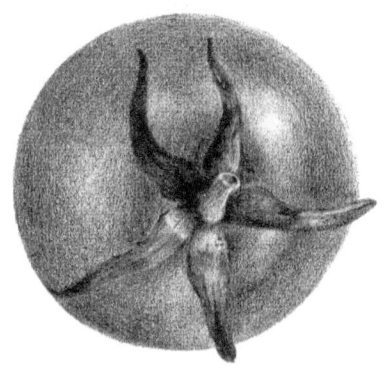

la luna di miele

you feed me *capperi*
from barrels of sea salt
little emeralds that hide
inside folds of pasta

I am hungry for
your *pomodoro* cheeks
singed *melanzane* hair
caponata lips
smooth as cream
the taste of smoke
blood of sauce

you feed me lemons
you stole from a tree
and squeeze them into
mineral water for me

satisfaction tastes like
fingers full of
chocolate hazelnut
skin of *marzapane*

now we are love
baked into *biscotti*
dipped into coffee

orange peels
splatter between
our fingers
like shooting stars
full of heaven

even the tomato is an immigrant

sailing from Peru
to land on the moon-faced pizza
whose crust rode hot winds of sirocco
heading north from Persia

the fusion of origins made for new tastes
experimental combinations
of voyage, imported itself

who knows how
the tomato became a sauce
what confusion it faced
what persecution

was it a revelation to Italian hands
who marveled at its nightshade flesh
did they bite its bulbous body
crying out in tart surprise
or was it so foreign
they tossed back into the sea
belonging nowhere

it's not easy to reinvent yourself
a refugee looking for a place to land
as my grandparents did
set adrift between worlds

il pomodoro might as well have
become blood
a golden apple from the garden
before anyone knew of sin
poised with shining seeds
to grow its vines in fresh soil

unaware it would
one day become impossible
to imagine a dish without it

il pomodoro

weak little vines,
how do you hold
this plump, juicy planet
of seeds that say I'm a fruit
but not always sweet

of tiny suns
sometimes yellow
camouflage
from watering mouths
who pretend
they are grapes and
burst on your tongue
like a firecracker

sometimes I feel like a tomato
wearing flesh that's ripe for kisses
whose unfinished insides
summon the sweet basil
of my olive oil lover
to invoke my flavors
and heat me to a boil

sometimes I feel
like a green cherry
worshipping the sky
until I'm sun-dried, shriveled
full of sensation and longing

until I am red
like an Italian woman's heart
until I am plump
like her lips and hips

I am juicy and dangerous
to eat or to cut
and I make a mess
splattering love and oceans
when you discover
the unpredictable
universe inside of me

secondi

where food comes from

dinner was Mother's pride
Sister's pride
they'd ask 5,000 times as you chew
    how is it?
        do you like it?
            is it good?
dishing out old favorites on a plate
    isn't this the best?
it's a rhetorical question
    whose sauce do you like better
    Mom's or mine?

they were so proud
I never really learned to cook
never helped in the kitchen
except set tables
clean dishes
finish my greens
mangia, mangia, mangia

I never knew where food came from
in the never ending asphalt of Brooklyn
only where recipes came from
    this is Mom's stuffed mushrooms
    Mother-in-Law's meatballs
    Brother-in-Law's clams in white wine sauce
all Italian
deep south
Sicily, Napoli
home of the famous pizza
which Mom would roll by hand
dusting the kitchen table with flour
pounded fresh dough
wet and cold from the local bakery

only my neighbor across the street
knew where food came from
when summer arrived
fingers full of earth
in her ten-foot square backyard
under the screeching train tracks
that would drown out the sound of birds

if I were lucky enough to be invited
into their private palace of fig trees
that would blossom in summer and transform
into garbage bag monsters in winter
I'd get to taste fresh tomatoes from the vine
and a watery, home made wine
which her father would make in his bath tub
 just a taste for the table, he'd say
and sometimes peppers, rosemary and basil grew
with enough sun along the side of their house
eggplants would bubble forth
in their nightshade secrecy
even a rogue pumpkin blossomed once
amongst alley cats and inch worms

living in the jungle city
has always left me longing
for the smell of freshly turned soil
to one day hold a plate of food
that I made with my bare hands
but none of these tiny patches of earth
belonged to us
crammed in a rental apartment
just lucky enough
to always have
an abundant table of food

a meal has never been just a meal
it was our past time
the reason to get together
occasions being secondary

everyone would call to ask
    so what are you making?
a month before they would arrive
looking forward to huddling around
a table too small for all the dishes of food
endless hours of yelling and eating
the same old dishes
the same old stories
over and over and over again

now that I am older and living out west
let loose among rows of organic vegetables
I've never seen before
ingredients from foreign lands
my parents never dreamed of going to
I wield my own adventures
over stove and table
traveling the uncharted territories of
India, Japan, China and Thailand

but if you ask me for my favorite dish
for what really satisfies my soul
I return to Italy
curving burnt corners of rolled *cannelloni*
stuffed artichokes brimming
with bread crumbs and *parmigiano* cheese
succulent bits of grilled *melanzane*
the time-tested dishes
from generations I've never known
but live forever
in the unwritten recipes
I've learned from my family

zucchini

in the space of a breath
I think about where you came from

I wonder which farm
from near or far
if you were loved
looked over with care
of the people it took to bring you to me
how long you had taken to grow

I think about the sun that touched you
the same sun that now touches me
makes everything grow
nourishes everything

I think about the soil you grew in
how many things have come
from that undying soil
how many things will grow again

of farmers who spend their mornings
working the land from sunrise to sunset
to fulfill my hunger

so much effort
    time
    patience
    sweat
    blood
    life
    death
in this moment
between me and
my forkful of zucchini

la cucina povera

never knowing what it's like to starve
to have the flame of hunger in their belly
they want to eat nothing but
la cucina povera
as if when they taste it
they will know the immediacy of life
the hunger and fire
that keeps us up at night
slaving for a crumb of bread

they want to eat the passions
of those who have nothing
but love
     like *peasant food*
that's dense and filling
quick to satiate
keep you rising at dawn
craving leftovers
singed at the edges
in unending circles of fire
cast among hot stones
     rustica
workers hands furiously beat
molded lips of pizza dough like clay
the burnt crust of *terraferma*
buried under ancient ash
     you scour
empty cupboards for a single spice
garlic cloves for *risotto*
mounds of *polenta*
funghi foraged from the hills
taste better than any fancy restaurant
serving peasant dishes we can not afford
to dressed up executives
who never had to cook a meal
to make sure no morsel is wasted

who do not know the precious cost of a grain
who pay top dollar for a simple dish
that will not satisfy your peasant soul
the way I can
missing the ingredient of our tears and sweat
made from what we can get our hands on
better when eaten with naked fingers

tastes like the kind of love
only a broken heart can feel
the heightened pleasure
felt by those who suffer

they go on
forever seek to emulate
what only we can taste
the blood of a tomato
sweat of the onion
flaming heart of artichoke
body of bread

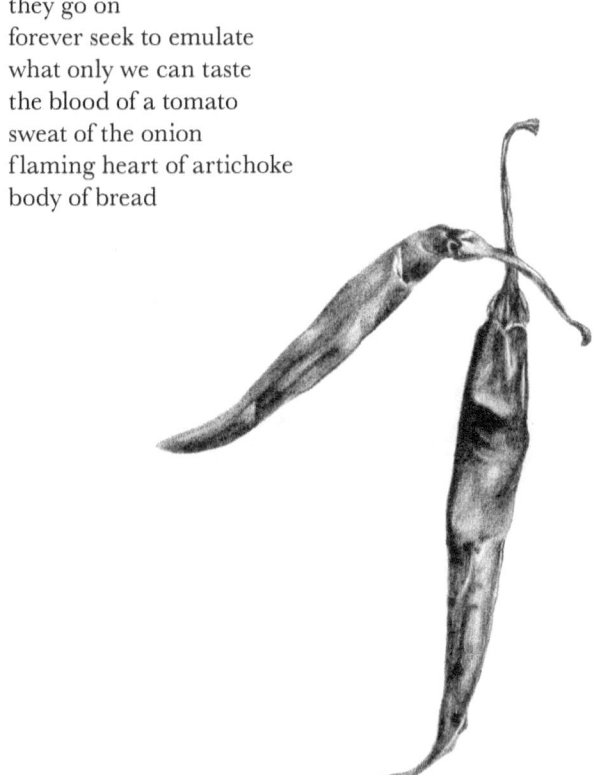

l'aglio

unravel her knot
and press
until she slips
hard to undress
that messy clove's
sheer negligee

some say she reeks
to high heaven
but to me
she is sweetly
wicked

flips between
fingers and knife
bounces off cutting boards
from parchment skin

stinks up the place

her white body
navigates hot pans
whole
split
spliced
diced
sizzled golden

leaves her pungent perfume
on fumbling fingers
courses through pores
intoxicating

infuses skin and senses
until you pass out
from her pervasive potion
powerful enough
to make vampires vacate

while for dessert
on double duty
she whips up
aphrodisiac induced lovers
with heated garlic loins
into fits of necking in the dark

il peperone

they want to crucify you on hot coals
sear your skin till it's as black as night
burn you until you become
crimson and sweet

inside you there is only space
scattered seeds of wisdom
white ribs trail an achilles tendon
to your conglomerate of stars

a nucleus of thoughts conjugate
    tie it up
stuff it with sound and goat cheese
an echo rings
inside your oblong heart

a chamber large enough
where we can stretch our palates
along waves of bulbous curves

I slice you into lipstick coated smiles
long and leggy strips
which crunch and crack between teeth

it could be
    my dear red pepper
you are more dangerous than an apple
full of subtle knowledge
but light as air

you fit gently inside my palm
when warmed with oil
you soften and lie
like a lover post-ecstasy
limp and lofty
across a bed of greens

free from the stem
that once tied you to the earth
full of the sun's fire

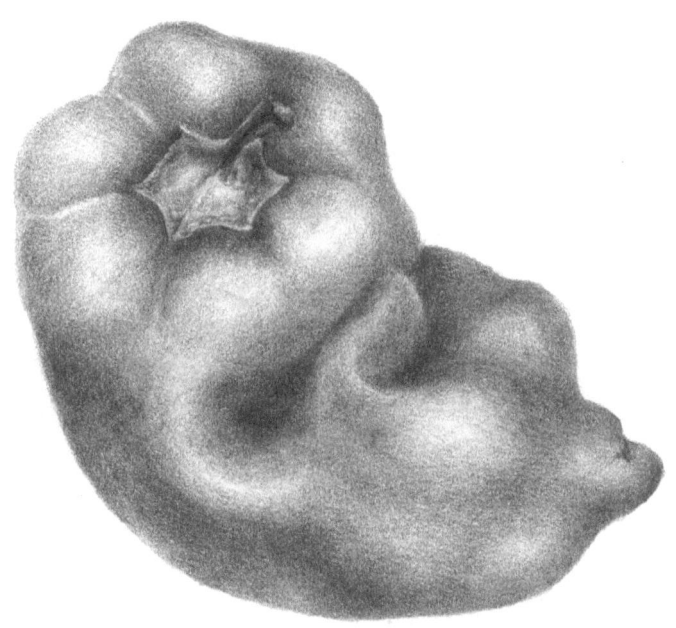

i pinoli

pine cone wings
unable to take flight
soar by the beak of
azure-winged magpies
who spread the precious
pearls of *pinoli*

from China and Syria
over hills of Greece
from the dust of Pompeii
they travel through time
into everything I make

I scatter them
copiously like confetti
sparing no expense
amongst bits of garlic
and olive oil they dance
popping as their cheeks burn
on the sides of my pan
until they crunch between teeth
exploding butter and wood

seemingly weightless
they are heavy with
a history of passion

pinoli grew
organs of love all over Rome
like Pinnochio's nose grew long
in the Middle East you must
eat one hundred before sleep
to stoke a fire between the sheets
Greeks mixed them
with honey and almonds
for three nights on end

but I just pretend
to like the way they
    adorn asparagus
       elevate salads from roughage
      top sweet cookies like jewels
their power hidden
in innocent pills
of secret love
I so often feed to you

la cipolla

do we evolve
like the onion
slowly
sometimes abruptly
peeled
by life's circumstances
narrowed to our core
of translucent honesty
disrobed layers
of porous skin
blood soaked muscles
throbbing and meaty
squishy mounds
of organs winding
the guts of a car engine
hot and steamy
tubes and links
that churn away
to skeleton bones
of soft ivory
and caramelized marrow
to cells buzzing in space
humming louder
to light
past white emptiness
in the end
and all throughout
able to cry
quickly
painfully
stripped to our sincerity
without pigment
tinting words and vision
never comfortable
or completely naked

only a thin layer
between us and the world
left to dissolve
until nothing
becomes everything
once more

dolce

l'affamato

a strange hunger comes over me
    to devour you
when you walk into the room

I wrap my arms and legs
around you
    koala-like
as if you were a fruit tree
I bite your cheeks
as if they were
    a nectarine

I can't tell if it's my
bottomless desire for love
or if I am simply

    hungry

your lips look like candy to me
your biceps like hunks of meat
I pretend to shake salt on your arm
and nibble you like an ear of corn

we must have learned this
when we were very young
suckling at our mother's breast
or on our thumb

even friends
with children say
how they are
    just so cute
    they want to eat them up
and call them names
of food stuff like
    muffin, sweet pea
and *my little peanut*

but *you*

I must love you so much
that being close

    is never close enough

I have a craving
to become one with all I love
and that must be why
I never feel satisfied

sensing in my appetite
this great illusion of separation

instead I dream
of your cheeks as dough
of your lips as cake
of my soul satiated
    for a moment
by the deliciousness
    of you

la prugna

you hand me
a plump, red plum
naked
on the living room floor
the sun beats down
on your ass
heats your hair red

my skin is flushed
my plum is tart
as teeth rip into it

taut like your stare
of mysterious thoughts
taking in perspiring pores
moans escape lips

I am your plum
after you bite
letting go of my juice
on your mouth
and the carpet

I am red
the rich flesh
of a rotund fruit

I am satisfied
after cells explode
the pulp of my plum
tiny bubbles that
burst on the tongue
carry sweet waters
to quench you
vibrate beyond form

fuck
the neighbors
must hate us
roll their eyes
enjoy our cries
in the midst of it
I don't care at all

I am nature
four elements and a fruit

I am earth and space

I am jelly
unable to move limbs

enjoying my plum
in the afterglow
and the shivers
that shake
my bones

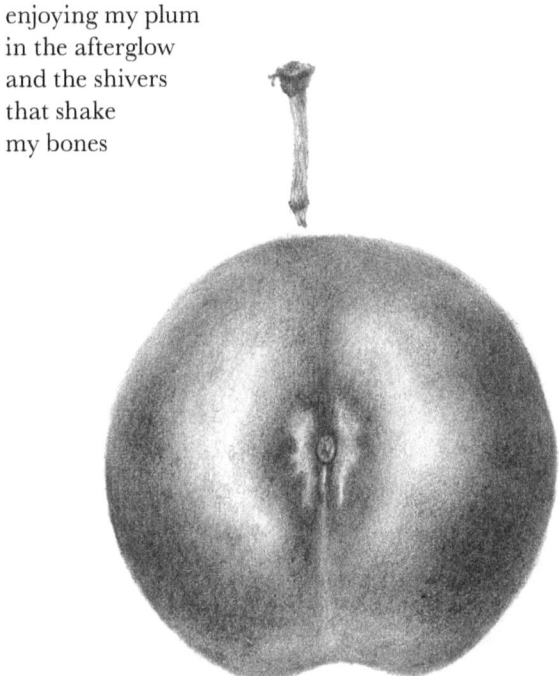

la passeggiata

in the morning
    sunrise
        biscotti, toast
crackers, *Nutella*
    cappuccino
        succo di frutta
arancia or passion fruit
    maybe a *cornetto*
        and nothing to do
except wander
    corners and crevasses
        ancient doorways loom
open and close the shutters
    laundry hanging limp
        on wires over the alley
terracotta tiles bake
    orange as the sun
        mopeds circle *la piazza*
forever puttering around
    until *pranzo*
        when doors say *chiuso*
the world stops
    at high noon
        for *antipasti*
a *primo* pasta
    and then *il secondo*
        from farm or sea
and then *il caffè*
    dolce
        and then
to make love
    a dormire
        a deep stupor
of too much pleasure

after 4 p.m.
    they start to stir
        to *fare una passeggiata*
as shops spill out
    onto the street
        selling their wares
of hand painted pottery
    books of fine leather
        coral jewels
eyes move side to side
    up and down
        the curve
of a woman's body
    on the street
        faces meet
eye to eye
    lips kiss cheeks
        from left to right
the human tide waves
    back and forth
        up and down
in and out
    until the shops
        close their shutters
and the last
    of the young lovers
        wander off looking
for a place to kiss
    under the moon

la pesca

your destiny is to fall
which may include
cutting your skin
on the pavement below
seeing orange blood
for the first time on your hands
the sweet taste of your self

oh, you would taste like a peach
and if you refuse to surrender
jaws will come
to pierce your fuzzy flesh
either way
your fate will only be
a moments pleasure on the palate
when forces of nature come
to have their certain way with you

should you fear
falling in love or to the earth
you might be immortalized as
still life with peaches or
nude with bowl of peaches
handpicked by
a discerning, artist lover
written into poetry like
ode to fruit flesh

should you shy away
grow heavy in the sun
slowly plump, unsatisfied
hoard your juices
trembling in the wind
out of reach of a lover who
looks up to you with hunger

your destiny will sadly be
to outgrow your lonely space
left rotting on the limb
like a wrinkled prune

oh, to be fearless
and follow your fate
baked into a nice pie or cake
covered with cream
initiated into desire
by a watering mouth
unexpectedly
an instrument used in
ecstatic rituals of love

such a destiny would be
worth the time
from seed to succulent fruit

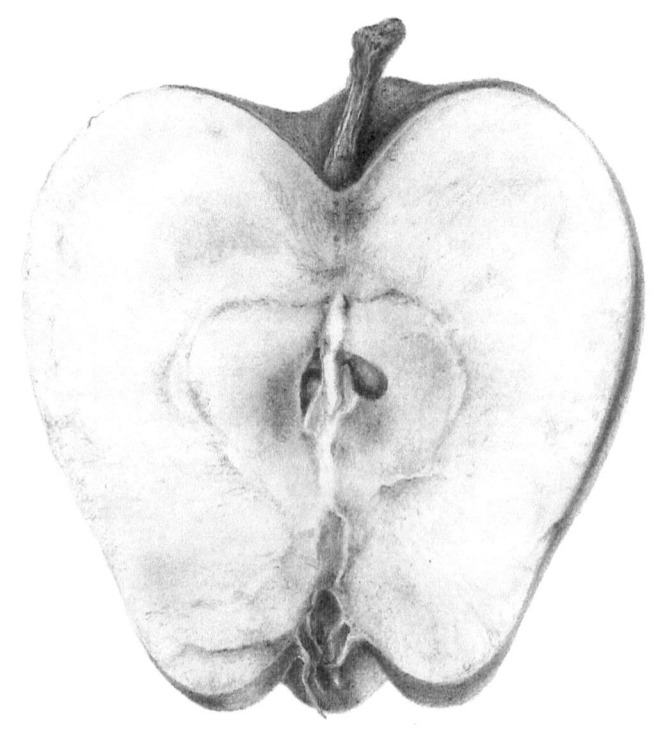

la mela

Eve bit down
she was tired of waiting around
she said *c'mon now, let's get this thing started*

it was a gleam
a whisper that became a scream
a half-moon bite that sparked
the circle of life

let's multiply

now they ask
if, when, how many?
as if I must bite
continue this feeding frenzy
that starts with apple sauce
moving on to wheat and meat
the fish, chicken and cows
all wait to eat and be eaten

on her orbital body we feed
rising from the fire in her belly
that breeds land and breathes trees
the apples fall like leaves

let's get this thing started

apples to an orange sun
twenty four hours in a circle combine
they're planting seeds of expectation
that will start and stop with me
two circular nipples and two breasts
you can imagine what's next

stop putting the pressure on
with appetites of continuity
I want to be free
of everything round
plump and juicy
of markets full of nectarines
of cantaloupe and aching seeds
the world is pumping out
delectable breeds

they ask me *if, when, why not?*
but I fear the question
more than the answer
I fear the carnage of the feast

Eve bit down
he bit and everyone bites
chewing off the sides
scrounging for our slice

but what's the price?

to one day become food for
the maggots and the magpies
returning to circle through
her womb again

because it was never
only Eve
really we are both
the apple and the seed

il nettare

    is it better to starve
    or to be allowed
    just a taste
    and then go on
    starving
    remembering
    that nectar

poet migration

it starts in the café
with a cup of coffee
    nursing it
in conversation
they sip
    they sip
        they sip slowly
some ask for extra foam
    for extra pleasure
they gather
    wings flap
some are slumped
heavily into chairs
others move their beaks
    to squawk and chatter
some won't let you
    get a word in
        edgewise
they fight over territory
start their mating dance
ask lots of questions
talk about
    desire
feathers ruffle violently
standing on tiptoe stilts
yell about conspiracies
bitch about the government
    will they ever tire
    bitching about the government?
they sip
    linger
        get restless
tear at crumbs
of cake and biscotti
weary of low, wooden seats

time to migrate
south

to the bar
for cheap beer and wine
they slowly peel themselves up
head out into the cold
one by one down the street
to a bar that's as old as the café
sell a book of poems
buy a beer
get into more conversation
more drinks
    more conversation
        chatter again
until the low mutter
becomes
boisterously LOUD
they go to the bathroom
out for a smoke
back in for a beer
bitch about the government
mating dance
ruffled feathers
until finally they tire

with little money left
it's time to go home
or back to the café

the slow migration
north
begins

il cappuccino

I order myself a cappuccino
in the middle of the day
in San Francisco

    sacrilege

cappuccino
traditionally savored
only in the morning in Italy
is served all day long
on this side of the globe
but *that* I don't mind
what I *do* mind is
cappuccino made bitter
by over burnt beans
watered
    way
        down
like the fog
that crosses the bay
and rolls over
the edge of my cup
with too much foam
not enough milk or sugar
to sweeten the taste

I suppose
in order to make it correctly
you need to honor its history

the cappuccino
was named after Saint Francis'
order of Capuchin friars
who refused to water down their order
and held steadfast to the rich, pure
ways of their sweet saint
unlike my cappuccino Americano
weakened by a lack of love
and the rush to get it to me quickly

oh no, Saint Francis would not approve
and definitely no self-respecting *Italiano*
I like my cappuccino like they do
which means
made with passionate care
    made right

the delicate brown swirl
of the cappuccino
received its name
from the color of the friars
hooded robes called a *cappuccio*

invented by a friar
who concocted
the first cappuccino
with foamed milk
and leftover honey
who swiftly staggered off
toward bigger miracles
like healing the sick
with one blessing

as for me
in the city of Saint Francis
in this day and age
all I want
is a decent cappuccino
    made properly
served in a small cup
    not too much foam
with an artfully swirled heart
atop its cappuccio

and to be
left in silence
    like the friars
to enjoy it

no life without

    sacrifice on the altar of the tongue
        its blood freshly metallic
hand over your blindfold, heart
        I depend on your breaking
        surge of bottomless longing
first suckle of the nipple
        became suckle of the popsicle
too bad the eyes
        are bigger than the mouth
I could devour the world
        and drain the Milky Way

il cioccolato

I want to be decadent
fire coursing through blood
bitter until you add your sweetness
whisked into an elixir
ready for transmission
from the Milky Way
once, as valuable as gold
traded for rabbits and sex
now more accessible than joy itself
and so, it pains and soothes
a dark friend in dark times
who comforts, who heals
satisfies momentary desires
that return on full moons
and late nights in between
fertile seed that plants
an amorous seed
hand-dipped harbinger
of love letters and
wet cherry
dripping down your fingers
if you feed it to me, I might say
I love you more than chocolate
but don't make me choose
when you're not looking
I'll fill a heart shaped box
with poems
and feed them to you
one by one

la dolce vita

I shall not postpone pleasure
I demand dessert take priority

let me eat cake

a thin layer of raspberry
where I lay my dreams
to take seed
this is how I live

sprinkling your flesh
with *Baci* kisses
I long
    for you
        never know
what may happen

I bless myself
with holy butterscotch
I sanctify the angel's food
with *gelati*
it's death by chocolate
where sinners burn
their gluttonous history

my idea of balance is
to eat savory selections
in small portions
so I may partake
in a sliver
of devil's food cake
    it's a misnomer

life serves up pleasure
after pleasure
for my personal
dolce vita

le ricette

mom's sauce

2 large cans of crushed, plum tomatoes
    Italian brands, imported from Italy are best
1 can of tomato paste
4 cloves of garlic, chopped
1 teaspoon of salt, 1 dash of black pepper to taste
1 tablespoon of sugar
2 tablespoons of dried oregano and basil
3 tablespoons of extra virgin olive oil
1/4 cup of dry, red wine (optional)

In a saucepan, sauté olive oil and garlic until tender. Add canned tomatoes, paste, sugar and seasonings. Stir, cover and simmer for 1 hour until sauce thickens. Add wine as it simmers.

mom's stuffed mushrooms

2 cups of bread crumbs seasoned with dried basil and oregano
1-2 cloves of minced garlic or 1 tablespoon of garlic powder
1 pound of button mushrooms
2 tablespoons of extra virgin olive oil, or more

Pre-heat the oven to 350 degrees. Clean and dry mushrooms, gently remove mushroom stems. In a separate bowl make a mixture of seasoned bread crumbs and garlic. Mix in olive oil until bread crumbs are slightly damp. Spoon stuffing into each mushroom cap with a teaspoon. Place mushrooms on an dry pan. Bake for 15-20 minutes, until brown and tender.

jennifer's pasta rustica

1 pound of farfalle pasta, cooked al dente
4 cloves of garlic, chopped
2 1/2 cups cherry or grape tomatoes, quartered or halved
1/2 cup of pine nuts
1 1/2 cups of mushrooms, sliced (optional)
3 tablespoons of extra virgin olive oil
1 teaspoon of salt
1 tablespoon of dried basil and oregano
1 cup of fresh mozzarella, diced
1/2 cup of fresh basil, chopped
grated Parmigiano cheese and fresh black pepper to taste

Sauté 2 tablespoons of olive oil and garlic until tender in an uncovered sauté pan. Add mushrooms and pine nuts until partially cooked. Add tomatoes and 1 tablespoon of olive oil. Season with salt, oregano, and dry basil flakes. Once cooked, add al dente pasta in the mix. Heat for two minutes, add mozzerella. Plate and garnish with fresh black pepper, grated cheese and top with fresh basil.

tommy's clams in white wine

4-5 cloves of garlic, chopped
1/2 cup of fresh parsley, chopped
2 cups of Pinot Grigio, dry white wine
3 tablespoons of extra virgin olive oil, or more
12 little neck clams: scrub the shells clean and let them sit for twenty minutes in a bowl of cool water to filter out sand.

Sauté olive oil, garlic and clams in a covered saucepan. Once garlic is tender, add white wine and a little more olive oil. Cover and steam until the clams begin to open. Once they open, add fresh parsley, a pinch of salt and it's ready to serve. Serve clams in a bowl, spoon over with broth. Garnish with fresh parsley and a side of rustic bread.

Note: the stuffing from "Mom's Stuffed Mushroom" recipe can also be used to make stuffed clams. Steam clams in water until they open. Remove top shell, stuff clams with stuffing, bake for ten minutes.

le note

Il Sale – The root of the word "salary" came from the Latin word for "salt." The phrase "worth your salt" came from Roman times when soldiers were paid in salt for their labor. Many cultures throughout history have valued salt so highly that violent battles were waged for access and control of salt and spices. "You are the salt of the earth" is a phrase from the bible in reference to those who believe in god.

Extra Virgin – In Roman mythology there was an epic battle between Minerva and Neptune for power in which they decided to settle their dispute with a contest to develop the most useful invention. Neptune created the horse but Minerva won when she developed the olive which can clearly be used in many ways.

I Fichi – The word *fichi* (figs) is an Italian slang term for a woman's vagina. I use it to describe a man's anatomy because of its similar shape and because it is filled with a million little seeds, (although you can claim that a woman's ovaries are too). The Hanging Gardens of Babylon and the Garden of Eden both had fig trees. Although most people know the story of Adam and Eve as having bitten into an apple because of an apple being depicted in famous paintings of the scene, it may have been a fig instead of an apple because the bible says they bit into "the fruit of the tree of knowledge" and immediately covered their bodies with fig leaves. The Buddha achieved enlightenment under the Bodhi tree (a Ficus religiosa) which was a fig tree.

The Poetry of Pasta – *Mangiamaccheroni* (the pasta eaters) was once a derogatory term for poor southerners who ate pasta on the street. Yet pasta transformed Naples, doubling its population thanks to its affordability and long shelf life. Torre del Greco (my family's town), is near Gragnano and Torre Annunziata, which became the first towns to industrialize and export pasta. As Italians emigrated to America, pasta – alongside pizza – became symbolic of "being Italian," with imported brands serving as a taste of home. Nearly every Italian town created its own pasta shape, and many names are now so common that few know their literal meanings – making it a pleasure to write this poem to reveal them.

Il Basilico – Both Adam and Eve wore fig leaves and Caesar wore laurel and olive branches in his hair, not basil. I imagine basil in this poem, poetic license.

You've Ruined My Pasta – Perfectly cooked pasta is never limp and is best cooked *al dente* – which means "to the teeth" because it is slightly hard when you bite it. Pasta usually goes bad or limp if it cooks too long and you do not pay attention to it, which is what happens if you are distracted.

Il Sugo – *Braciole* is a dish made of thin beef rolled with cheese and raisins, cooked in a tomato sauce. *Arancini* are Sicilian rice balls stuffed with cheese or meat and sauce, then covered in flour and deep fried. Most Italians make sauce with canned or jarred tomatoes, but I like to make a rustic sauce with fresh cherry tomatoes too.

La Luna di Miele – "Honeymoon", written during our honeymoon in Sicily, highlights the ingredients we ate – many of which are staples of Sicilian cooking. Although we were married on the island of Capri, off the coast of Naples, a place with a rich history of poets including Pablo Neruda, who wrote The Captain's Verses there. Lam, the artist of this book, officiated our ceremony.

Where Food Comes From – "*Mangia, mangia!*" is a phrase Italian mothers use when they want you to finish your food. In Italy, the greatest gift to a chef is an empty plate and a request for seconds. This poem is about my neighbors in Brooklyn, NY – mostly southern Italian emigrants – who often grew traditional Italian ingredients in their gardens. Fig trees were wrapped in black garbage bags and tied with rope to survive the winter snow. In most Italian homes, the food Mom makes is the centerpiece, and the dinner table is a main focus of conversation and activity during the holidays.

La Cucina Povera – This term means "peasant food" or food of the poor. It is ironic that the dishes we see in the most expensive Italian restaurants in America are typically dishes associated with *la cucina povera*. These dishes consist of rustic food made with seasonal ingredients that could be easily foraged from the hillsides for free and made with ample and affordable ingredients such as: polenta with mushrooms, risotto, pasta and pizza.

La Passeggiata – *Fare una passeggiata* (taking a walk) is one of the major pastimes in Italy. After a big meal, people stroll up and down the main street to mingle and "walk it off." They gather in *la piazza*, the main square at the center of town. It's a healthy practice, but also a philosophy of life – and one of my favorite things to do in Italy.

La Mela – In the bible it says that Eve bites a "fruit from the tree of knowledge." Although it does not mention an apple, the apple has been the fruit depicted in famous paintings of this moment in the Garden of Eden. I find it interesting that a bite into the fruit of wisdom would spark the multiplicity of life. In yoga philosophy, the first of the 5 Koshas is called the "Annamaya Kosha" which means the "food layer" representing the physical body as one of the layers that separates us from a core of bliss and our natural state of oneness. I use the apple to discuss the pressures of being a woman, able to conceive and continue the cycle of life where we come from food and into food we return.

I Pinoli, L'Aglio – It's not surprising to me that Italians are known for being great lovers, such as the world famous *Casanova*. Most of the basic ingredients in Italian cuisine are love-inducing, natural aphrodisiacs such as garlic, pine nuts, chocolate, coffee, seafood, wine etc...the list goes on and on...another reason why I love Italian food so much.

mille grazie

To my family for raising me on Italian food and love, Daniel Heffez for encouraging me and for being my muse – *ti amo*. Lam Khong for his fine art and inspiration for the many details of this book, but most of all for his great friendship. Ingrid Keir at *Feather Press* for taking her editorial eye to these tasty poems and for being *la mia famiglia*. Joanna Tumminia, Lisa Engelken and Valentina Ottiano for refining my Italian language studies and my fellow poets in San Francisco who are great friends and an inspiration to me, always.

Grazie for letting me feature some of these poems in public and in print: Joseph Carboni at *Libreria Pino / Telegraph Hill Books,* Jack Hirschman, Kim Shuck, and the *San Francisco Public Library, SF Istituto Italiano di Cultura, SF Italian Consulate, Museo Italo Americano,* Tony Gemignani at *Giovanni's, The Red Poppy Art House:* the first to allow me to host a poetry & food night, Andrew Paul Nelson, Caitlyn Skye Wild & friends at *Golden Sardine & Coit Tower Poetry Club,* Jessica Loos & Dan Macchiarini at *First Fridays,* Jerry Ferraz & Eric Whittington at *Bird & Beckett Books,* Avotcja at *KPOO,* Dan Brady at *Sacred Grounds,* Jerry Cimino and Bob Booker at *The Beat Museum, Alley Cat Books, Book Passage, Adobe Books, The Gardener,* Jonathan Siegel at *Viracocha,* René Vaz, Marguerite Munoz at *Voz Sin Tinta,* Evan Karp and friends at *LitSeen* and *Quiet Lightning,* Genny Lim at *SFJazz Center,* Stephen Kopel, Clara Hsu & John Rhodes at *Clarion Music* and *SF Poetry TV,* Alice Rogoff & Cesar Love at the *Haight Ashbury Literary Journal,* Nicole Savage at *SF Heart,* Bill Mercer at *La Promenade Cafe,* Diamond Dave and Val Ibarra at *Mutiny Radio,* Jeanne Lupton at *Frank Bette Center for the Arts,* Charlie Getter & J. Brandon Loberg at the *16th & Mission Street Review,* James Zealous & Bloodflower at *Kassidat,* Kevin Brown at *Live Worms Gallery,* E.K. Keith, Ginger Murray, Sarah Page, Steven Gray, Guinevere Q., Tracy Jones, Adrian Arias, Cara Vida & Sal, Pablo Rosales, Martin Hickel, Phillip T. Nails, David Madgalene, Marc Kockinos, Sara Marinelli, Shideh Etaat at *Hazel Reading Series,* Philip Hackett at *The Poet's Gallery,* Daniel Yaryan at *Sparring with Beatnik Ghosts* and many, many more ... *Grazie!*

jennifer barone

Jennifer is an Italian-American poet, born in Brooklyn, New York, with roots in the Bay of Naples, Italy. She travels Italy extensively, studies *la bella lingua* and currently resides in North Beach, San Francisco, a neighborhood known for its Italian heritage and a lineage of poets and artists. She is a two-time winner of the 2012 and 2007 SF Public Library's *Poets Eleven* contest for North Beach. She has been a featured poet at most local venues for poetry, and the host of *The WordParty Poetry and Jazz Series*. She has been published in literary journals such as *The Marin Poetry Center Anthology, Colossus Press Current: Water Journal, Forum Literary Magazine of CCSF, The Haight Ashbury Literary Journal, Quiet Lightning: Sparkle & Blink, Accolades: A WWS Anthology*, and two *Poets 11 Anthologies* by the SF Public Library. To learn more, visit: **jenniferbarone.wordpress.com** and follow: **@baronejenn**

She has had the great privilege to know Lam Khong, whom she first met in NY while exhibiting his art in the 90's. Since then they have shared many travels and conversations about love and art over the years, usually over a table of delicious food.

lam khong

Lam studied at the Dominican School of Philosophy and Theology; received his BFA from the College of Santa Fe, and MFA in Rome, Italy, through American University. He has participated in group and solo exhibitions in the United States and abroad including Berkeley, Boston, Denver, Florida, New York, Rome, and Santa Fe.

He says, *"Jennifer and I are dear friends of over twenty years. We have shared tears and laughter over many memorable meals, celebrating life and succo d'amore. I am happy to have been asked to be a part of her project. I would love to cook everyone a good dinner. Here, Jennifer and I are serving up some food and love through our poetry and art for you. Tante belle cose."*

www.ingramcontent.com/pod-product-compliance
Lightning Source LLC
Chambersburg PA
CBHW032053290426
44110CB00012B/1073